The Urbana Free Library

To renew materials call
217-367-4057

	DATE DUE		

WITH AND WITHOUT

BY JEFFREY SWEET

★

★

DRAMATISTS
PLAY SERVICE
INC.

for Kristine

WITH AND WITHOUT was produced by Victory Gardens Theater (Dennis Zacek, Artistic Director) in Chicago, Illinois, on November 10, 1995. It was directed by Sandy Shinner; the set design was by Bill Bartelt; the costume design was by Margaret Morettini; the lighting design was by Chris Phillips; and the production stage manager was Christi-Anne Sokolewicz. The cast was as follows:

JILL	Annabel Armour
MARK	James Sherman
SHELLY	Linnea Todd
GLEN	Mark Vann

WITH AND WITHOUT was produced on the radio by WFMT's Chicago Theatres on the Air (Susan Albert Loewenberg, Executive Producer), in association with Victory Gardens Theater (Dennis Zacek, Artistic Director) in Chicago, Illinois, on April 13, 1995. It was directed by Sandy Shinner. The cast was as follows:

JILL	Lindsay Crouse
MARK	Michael Tucker
SHELLY	Jill Eikenberry
GLEN	Tim Halligan

WITH AND WITHOUT received its premiere in a workshop production by Artistic New Directions, in association with, and at the Frog Pond Theater in Upper Jay, New York, on July 15, 1994. It was directed by Michael Gellman. The cast was as follows:

JILL	Kristine Niven
MARK	Dan Daily
SHELLY	Beth Lincks
GLEN	Erol (K.C.) Landis

ACKNOWLEDGMENT

The author would like to express his appreciation to Beth Lincks and Kristine Niven for their improvisational participation in the development of this script.

The author would like to thank Judith Royer, who provided a valuable perspective directing early readings as part of the developmental process at Alice's Fourth Floor.

Acknowledgments

WITH AND WITHOUT

SCENE ONE

On a deck of a country house, overlooking a lake. A door leads into the house. The deck also has steps down that provide access to a path around the side of the house. Summer, late afternoon. At rise, Mark and Jill are on the deck. They are in their mid thirties to late forties. Mark is dressed casually. Jill, dressed in city clothes, is fiddling with a Nerf gun.

JILL. No, if he shows he'll just show.

MARK. Did he say he might? When you talked to him?

JILL. Mark, this isn't on the basis of talking to him. This is on the basis of living with him. Years of experience and acquired — *(A beat. She fires the Nerf gun at Mark. One of the sponges hits or lands near him.)* I've figured out how it works. Aren't I clever?

MARK. I never said otherwise.

JILL. You gonna give that back?

MARK. So you can shoot at me again?

JILL. Doesn't hurt.

MARK. Maybe I just don't want to be a target.

JILL. Where did this come from?

MARK. People we're renting from have a kid. Probably left it out by accident.

JILL. No, Russ will either show up or he won't show up. And probably even he doesn't know. And probably he won't know until he finds himself here, or doesn't. He'll just open the door to his car and say, "Oh, look where I am!"

MARK. And act accordingly.

JILL. Or not. He's Russ. Never can tell.

MARK. I'm sorry, Jill.

JILL. Of course you are. I'm gonna change. *(As Jill begins her exit, Shelly, about the same age as Mark and Jill, enters from the house carrying a wicker hamper.)*

SHELLY. I've finished putting the stuff away.

JILL. Back in a sec. *(Jill exits. Shelly perches on the deck.)*

SHELLY. God damn Russ. Now I'm going to have to make the pasta instead of the roast.

MARK. What does that have to do with Russ?

SHELLY. Well, *dinner* —

MARK. Yeah?

SHELLY. It doesn't spontaneously generate out of the collective will. "Oh, we're hungry." Bang — there's dinner. It has to be made.

MARK. Yes.

SHELLY. If we were going to eat at seven, I'd have to put the roast in right now for it to be done.

MARK. At seven.

SHELLY. That's how long it takes. But we don't know if we're *going* to eat at seven because we don't know if Russ will show up by then. Pasta, on the other hand —

MARK. It's faster.

SHELLY. He shows up, I can have pasta ready like ten, fifteen minutes later. I can't have the roast ready —

MARK. No, I grasp the concept. *(Shelly has pulled a bottle of wine and two wine glasses out of the hamper and poured Mark a glass.)* Thanks. The thing is, we don't know if he's going to show up at all.

SHELLY. Oh, I thought it was a "when" question. But it's "if"?

MARK. Yeah.

SHELLY. *(Getting the implications.)* Oh.

MARK. Yeah. *(A beat.)*

SHELLY. So, you and Jill have a good talk?

MARK. Mmmm.

SHELLY. No?

MARK. Well, I want to be there for her, of course.

SHELLY. Of course.

MARK. *(Nodding.)* On the other hand, I don't want to say anything that will suddenly throw her into — I didn't want her to — to start crying, 'cause then you're supposed to step forward and do that thing —

SHELLY. Which?

MARK. You know, a pat on the back, or hold her.

SHELLY. You don't want that to happen?

MARK. To hold her? No, I really don't. But if she starts crying, what are you going to do? Just stand there and make sympathetic noises?

SHELLY. What's a sympathetic noise?

MARK. You know.

SHELLY. Make me a sympathetic noise. So if I hear it in the future I can identify it.

MARK. "Ohhhhh." Or, "there, there."

SHELLY. "There, there?"

MARK. "There, there."

SHELLY. Oh yes, that would help a lot. "There, there." I'll have to remember that.

MARK. What really *does* help?

SHELLY. It's hard being a sensitive man, isn't it?

MARK. You think I'm not a sensitive man?

SHELLY. I think you're a *very* sensitive man. That's what you want to be, right?

MARK. Yeah, but, you know, in a manly way. Stoic, but in my eyes you can read deep reservoirs of —

SHELLY. Feeling.

MARK. Yes. That's what I'm shooting for. That's my goal.

SHELLY. So what are you afraid of?

MARK. Afraid?

SHELLY. With Jill? That if she, in a fit of whatever, propelled herself into your arms — that what?

MARK. That it might throw a switch onto a track we used to travel down that isn't appropriate to travel down now.

SHELLY. Meaning what? That you'll suddenly have this overwhelming urge to start pawing at her clothes?

MARK. Shelly —

SHELLY. Or the other way round?

MARK. Well, don't you sometimes, when you run into old boyfriends —

SHELLY. There are so many of them —

MARK. I'm saying when you do, on those rare occasions when you *do*, don't you sometimes find old impulses being triggered?

SHELLY. Not triggered. Remembered. Acknowledged.

MARK. Unh-hunh.

SHELLY. Well, of course remembered. I don't forget people. I don't forget that something happened, if something happened.

MARK. But there's a difference between like remembering, oh, "once upon a time this person and I" — so forth and so on — between *that,* which is an intellectual thing — "I know this" — your word: "acknowledge" — between that and the feelings themselves coming back. Echoes of them.

SHELLY. And if she weren't around you wouldn't have to cope with these echoes?

MARK. May I point out something here? Let me point something out. And I'm casting no particular, uh, castings, which is that you're the reason she —

SHELLY. She what?

MARK. You were the one who made the big gesture of "I don't care what happened between you and Mark in the past —"

SHELLY. I didn't. Why should I?

MARK. Not saying you should. But to say, pretty much, "I want you to be a friend of the family." Which I thought was a lovely gesture and much appreciated. And a lot of women wouldn't have done that.

SHELLY. Hey, you're sensitive, I'm noble.

MARK. But you, in a way, have made her more welcome into our lives than I think I would have?

SHELLY. Do you *not* want her in our lives?

MARK. I'm just saying that having her in our lives is not always easy.

SHELLY. And you only want friends who are easy.

MARK. It's kind of nice when you're on vacation, yeah. Last

time I looked, that's what this was supposed to be. We've got all the fixings — the lake here, a bunch of silly board games — I brought along three paperback novels with guns on the cover. After all the bullshit in the office, I came up here in anticipation of a certain kind of week by way of contrast. And instead —

SHELLY.   What is it? Are you afraid if she hugs you you're going to get hard?

MARK.   I'm so glad we can have these conversations.

SHELLY.   Well, you said triggers. What other triggers could you be talking about? You ever think about her naked any more? What she looks like?

MARK.   I don't know what she *looks* like. It's been years.

SHELLY.   What she *looked* like then. Come on, fess up.

MARK.   What is the point of asking this question?

SHELLY.   You do, don't you? Remember?

MARK.   I really don't see the point of asking —

SHELLY.   You do, don't you?

MARK.   You're just trying to make me blush.

SHELLY.   The perils of being a sensitive man. It's OK if you do, you know — remember.

MARK.   Let me get this straight: I have your *permission?*

SHELLY.   You do it anyway, don't you? *I* do.

MARK.   Oh, you think about Jill naked?

SHELLY.   You know what I'm saying.

MARK.   I know what you're saying. *Why* you're saying it — that's another matter.

SHELLY.   Would you look at your shoulders?

MARK.   What about them?

SHELLY.   They're up around your ears.

MARK.   And this signifies what?

SHELLY.   OK, OK, I'll stop.

MARK.   Who do *you* think about naked?

SHELLY.   Never mind.

MARK.   Oh, it's OK for you to razz me but —

SHELLY.   I did have a life before I met you.

MARK.   Is there someone in particular? Or do you mentally skip around between erotic highlights?

SHELLY.   I *had* no erotic highlights until you came along.

MARK.   I believe you.

SHELLY.   Give me your lips.

MARK.   You want them so bad, come get them. *(Shelly goes over to him and kisses him with serious intention. The kiss ends.)* More, more, I'm still not satisfied. *(Shelly gives him a playful swat, puts her finger to her lips and nods in the direction of the inside to indicate that she hears Jill returning. Jill enters in casual clothes.)* You changed — nice.

SHELLY.   Jill, something to drink? We brought some wine up. *(Shelly pulls a third glass out of the hamper.)*

MARK.   One of Shelly's clients, every Christmas, sends over a case, practically.

JILL.   Fine.

SHELLY.   It's pretty good stuff.

JILL.   Fine. Sure.

MARK.   *(Pours.)* This is supposed to have a wonderful bouquet. I don't know what that means really. Tell me. *Does* this have a wonderful bouquet?

JILL.   Yes. It also has good legs. *(Shelly laughs.)*

MARK.   Is that actually a real thing?

JILL.   Look, you see, you hold it up to the light, you tilt the glass a little. Now, you see where it's falling down on the sides? If it clings to the glass, it has good legs.

MARK.   I'm astonished. Shelly, your wine could be a Rockette.

JILL.   This is actually very nice.

SHELLY.   Could I have some more, too?

MARK.   Oh yes, sorry. Of course. *(Pours.)*

JILL.   Somebody should call Russ.

MARK.   Why?

JILL.   Well, for the obvious reason it would be nice to know if he's coming. Somebody should call him.

MARK.   Why do you look at me when you say "somebody?"

JILL.   Come on, Mark.

MARK.   And what is this hypothetical somebody supposed to say?

SHELLY.   That we're preparing dinner and we want to know

if he's going to join us for it. Or, if he's coming late, should we tell him where we're going to be —

MARK.   Are we going out?

SHELLY.   If we want to go out.

MARK.   Perfect. You know what to say, you've got the job.

JILL.   I think it's better if you do it.

MARK.   Why is it better if I do it?

JILL.   Because you're a guy.

MARK.   What?

JILL.   Well, you *are.*

MARK.   I'm not disputing that. I'm disputing that my being a guy has anything to do with why it's more appropriate for me to make this call.

JILL.   Well, you're a guy, he's a guy, you've got a guy friendship, you and Russ —

MARK.   Why is it that two guys — any two guys, any two heterosexual guys — are supposed to be able to talk in a way that — I think this idea is a complete fallacy. No pun intended. *(Jill laughs in spite of herself.)*

JILL.   You are so —

MARK.   *(Overlapping.)* I don't play racquetball with him. I don't go drinking with him. If you added up all the time I have spent alone with him since you two got married —

JILL.   Don't you like him?

MARK.   I like him OK, but he wouldn't be my friend if he weren't married to you.

SHELLY.   Why not? He's *my* friend.

MARK.   All right, yes, he would have been my friend because he's *your* friend. *(To Jill.)* But the fact of the matter is, now he's married to you, and because he's married to you — that's the reason he comes into our life. That's why he'd be here this week, why we've been together other weeks, because of you being a couple. Because these weeks are about two couples sharing this kind of time.

JILL.   I still think you should call.

SHELLY.   I do, too.

MARK.   Excuse me, this is not up to a vote.

JILL.   Why won't you?

MARK. He's gonna know that I'm calling not just to find out, "Are you coming up?" And what if he says he's *not* going to come? What then?

JILL. You could ask why.

MARK. See, the thing is, if I do that, he might tell me.

JILL. No, I know what: you should tell him — this is perfect — you should tell him *I* haven't shown up.

SHELLY. You?

JILL. I haven't shown up and you're worried about me.

MARK. But how would we know that you were going to be coming up in a different car from him?

JILL. I called while I was on the road and told you so. Told you that I was on the way.

MARK. Why would you call us on the road?

JILL. I was passing the store in town and wondered if there was something I could pick up for dinner. And so you were expecting me in a few minutes, but that was more than an hour ago and where could I be? Has he heard anything?

SHELLY. So he thinks maybe you've been in an accident?

JILL. Whatever he wants to think. Whatever conclusion he wants to —

SHELLY. But that's a lie.

JILL. I'm not saying you should tell him that I've *been* in an accident.

SHELLY. But to say that you haven't shown up.

JILL. Right.

SHELLY. But you *have* shown up.

MARK. You're right here. I see you.

JILL. A technicality.

MARK. The truth is a technicality.

SHELLY. How would you feel if we did something like that to you?

JILL. How would I know?

SHELLY. You could find out. Whenever someone does stuff like this —

MARK. — people find out.

SHELLY. Thank you, I really wanted that sentence finished.

JILL. No, you're right. It was a stupid idea. Besides, Mark

couldn't pull it off.

MARK. Gee, I think I'm offended.

SHELLY. You're offended that she says you're not a liar.

MARK. That's not what she's saying. She's saying I don't have the talent to *be* one. That choice of whether or not to lie — that's a moral question. The *ability* to lie — that speaks to competence. She's saying that I'm not competent.

JILL. All right, forget it.

MARK. Thank you, I will.

JILL. But I still think someone should call.

SHELLY. All right, I'll call.

MARK. And what are you going to say?

SHELLY. "Shall we expect you for dinner or not? Are you going to be late?"

MARK. Sounds excellent.

JILL. And if he says he's not coming, ask him why. And maybe what her name is.

MARK. Her name?

JILL. Whoever the bimbo is he's —

MARK. *(To Shelly.)* Unh-hunh, see?

SHELLY. *(To Jill.)* Are you sure you don't want to call yourself?

JILL. The whole point is what he'd say to you. I know what he'd say to me. He's said it.

MARK. But you want Shelly to ask what *you* want her to ask. Maybe you should be in the same room? Hold up cuecards for the conversation?

JILL. Don't talk to me like that.

MARK. Sorry. *(To Shelly.)* But I think if you *do* get him on the phone, the conversation's going to turn to something beyond is he or isn't he going to come up here. And do you want to be part of that conversation?

SHELLY. Well, it's preferable to this one.

MARK. Do you want him to say something to you under pressure that might be irrevocable? Do you want to be the one to have to bring the news of that back?

SHELLY. I'm going to call. I will say what I think needs to be said. *(She goes inside.)*

JILL. You chicken. You're such a chicken.

MARK. Thank you.

JILL. You've always been a chicken.

MARK. Thank you.

JILL. Well, you *have*.

MARK. That's right. Aren't you glad you didn't end up with a chicken?

JILL. If you'd ended up with me, you wouldn't have been a chicken.

MARK. By definition.

JILL. Well, it's true, isn't it?

MARK. Absolutely, yes, it's true.

JILL. Well, it is.

MARK. I'm not going to disagree with you.

JILL. You're too chicken to disagree with me.

MARK. Probably.

JILL. You're so tentative, so fucking cautious.

MARK. If you mean I don't dive into a swimming pool unless I'm sure there's water in it —

JILL. You don't dive into a swimming pool unless it's heated to precisely seventy-eight point two degrees.

MARK. Excuse me, are you insulting me?

JILL. Of course I'm insulting you.

MARK. Just checking.

JILL. What the fuck do you *think* I'm doing?

MARK. No, if I have a choice between being called an asshole and someone who likes to swim in a warm pool —

JILL. Oh, shut up.

MARK. On the other hand, if you'd called me a Rush Limbaugh fan —

JILL. Stop being rational! God damn, I'm so tired of that tone —

MARK. What tone?

JILL. You explaining the ramifications of everything. Don't you ever have an impulse? Or did you have it removed surgically —

MARK. What?

JILL. Whatever organ or gland it is that secretes impulses,

16

spur of the moments?

MARK. I think you mean spurs of the moment.

JILL. Stop it! Just stop it! *(Shelly returns.)*

SHELLY. What's he doing?

MARK. Being too rational.

SHELLY. *(Offhandedly.)* Yeah, that's annoying, stop it.

JILL. So?

SHELLY. I left a message on his machine.

JILL. How many rings? Two or four?

MARK. What difference does that make?

SHELLY. Toll-saver.

MARK. What's that?

SHELLY. It's a feature on some answering machines. You put it on toll-saver, if there are messages waiting, it rings twice before it answers. If there are no messages, it rings four times.

MARK. So, if it rang four times, what would that mean?

JILL. It would mean that he's picked up my messages. That what I said wasn't enough to get him to call me here. It was four rings, right?

SHELLY. I'm sorry.

JILL. Well, no, it just gives me more information to work with. He heard my messages, he erased them, he didn't call here. It gives me a better idea where I stand.

MARK. I don't see how that's necessarily true.

JILL. You know, your opinion on this is real valuable.

SHELLY. Hey now —

JILL. Can I have another glass? *(To Mark.)* Don't look at me like that. It's wine. *(Shelly picks up bottle and pours Jill another glass.)*

SHELLY. So, are you up for linguini? *(Lights out.)*

SCENE TWO

An hour or so later. Sunset. Mark is alone on the deck. Shelly enters.

MARK.   You know what we could do.

SHELLY.   What?

MARK.   Leave.

SHELLY.   Just do that, hunh?

MARK.   Yeah.

SHELLY.   Leave?

MARK.   Toss our stuff into the back of the car, hit the road —

SHELLY.   Say goodbye or not?

MARK.   Maybe wave to her. Jill's still on the phone, right?

SHELLY.   Still, yes.

MARK.   Good. She's on the phone, we wave, "See you." When she finally gets off the phone, in a couple hours, she realizes that we didn't mean "see you later," we meant "see you — "

SHELLY.   "Much later."

MARK.   We could be back to the city in time for *Charlie Rose*. Have a glass of wine. Congratulate each other over a narrow escape.

SHELLY.   And what would she do?

MARK.   That would be up to her. She's an adult.

SHELLY.   Drink?

MARK.   Probably.

SHELLY.   Cry?

MARK.   She's gonna do that whether we're here or not. I mean, she's mapped out this week for misery. The question is whether it's solo or communal.

SHELLY.   And the money we blew to rent this place? We kiss that off?

MARK.   The point of this was to spend a nice relaxing week with our friends. Since only fifty percent of our friends showed

18

up, and she is not making for a relaxing time —

SHELLY. Her feelings would be badly hurt.

MARK. On the other hand, we might reach the end of the week alive. *(A beat.)*

SHELLY. You're not serious.

MARK. Of course not.

SHELLY. You're just saying this in the spirit of — what?

MARK. Yeah. Exactly.

SHELLY. Irony.

MARK. That, too.

SHELLY. A little sardonic humor to cover the compassion you really feel.

MARK. You've got me nailed. That's me.

SHELLY. How soon do you want to leave?

MARK. You're kidding, right?

SHELLY. Yeah.

MARK. Damn.

SHELLY. We can't.

MARK. I know.

SHELLY. We *can't.*

MARK. I know we can't.

SHELLY. Damn.

MARK. You want me to rub your neck?

SHELLY. You think it needs it?

MARK. It's so knotted up it looks like a piece of challah. Come on — sit. *(Shelly sits in front of Mark, who begins to rub her neck.)*

SHELLY. I envy bastards.

MARK. How so?

SHELLY. It must be so liberating. Like — who is it? "Now is the winter of our discontent —"

MARK. Richard III.

SHELLY. You remember Olivier in the movie? How much fun he had? All that twinkling evil. "This is what I'm gonna do." Murder, seduction, betrayal. Those two kids. No apologies, no scruples, no hesitations. Just blast away.

MARK. Of course he died at the end.

SHELLY. Of course he died. In the classics, there has to be

balance, justice. Classical literature — he *has* to be punished.

MARK. As opposed to real life?

SHELLY.   Hey, Franco died of old age. So did J. Edgar Hoover. So did my grandma Ruth. You never met her.

MARK.   And I am thankful for it.

SHELLY.   Mean. And never pretended to be anything but.

MARK.   What was her excuse? The Depression?

SHELLY.   She didn't make any excuse. If you had something and she wanted it, she'd say, "Give me that." And if you asked why, she'd say, "Because I want it more than you." And she did. She wanted Grandpa. He was married to someone else. So what. She wanted him, she got him, and once she got him, she made his life miserable.

MARK.   You've inherited genes from this person?

SHELLY.   It was like she figured out that if she got rid of her conscience there wouldn't be any friction.

MARK.   Friction?

SHELLY.   Yeah. I mean, let's say you have the impulse to do something, something crummy. Like, "Oh, I'd like to ram that jerk in the red car." You'd do it — right? — if it weren't for friction.

MARK.   You're talking moral friction?

SHELLY.   Some voice — some Elmer Fudd voice that pops up with things to consider. Like fairness, or other people's safety or feelings, or the rule of law.

MARK.   Yours sounds like Elmer Fudd?

SHELLY.   What does yours sound like?

MARK.   John Houseman.

SHELLY.   Ooooh.

MARK.   What's that smell?

SHELLY.   Over there — that guy is barbecuing. *(Mark picks up binoculars.)*

MARK.   Yup. Oh, he's wearing one of those joke barbecue things.

SHELLY.   What, aprons?

MARK.   Yeah.

SHELLY.   What's it say? What's the joke?

MARK.   I can't see. Something about meat. Something about

eating meat.

SHELLY.   Thank you, I get the idea.

MARK.   You want to look?

SHELLY.   What I want is your hands.

MARK.   You got it. *(He puts down the binoculars and returns to rubbing her neck. Shelly begins to moan from the neck rub.)* Does that mean that feels good?

SHELLY.   Mmmmm.

MARK.   How come I never hear that sound in bed?

SHELLY.   You should rub my neck in bed.

MARK.   Thank you very much. *(He stops rubbing her neck.)*

SHELLY.   Oh come on, a joke.

MARK.   Yeah, well there've been a lot of jokes like that flying around here tonight. Jokes of that ilk.

SHELLY.   What ilk?

MARK.   It's kind of a therapeutic thing, right?

SHELLY.   What is?

MARK.   She makes a crack, you make a crack, I'm supposed to be a good sport. Laugh along.

SHELLY.   You think we're picking on you?

MARK.   On what I represent.

SHELLY.   Oh? What do you represent?

MARK.   People with dicks.

SHELLY.   You represent them, do you? All of them?

MARK.   Not of my choosing. But, since I am the one person in the vicinity at the moment who matches that description, I seem to have been elected by default.

SHELLY.   It must be a burden.

MARK.   Just because Russ and I have this one anatomical characteristic in common doesn't mean that we share other characteristics as well.

SHELLY.   *(Intending it as a joke.)* Well, you're all no damn good.

MARK.   That's supposed to be funny, right?

SHELLY.   Oh, come on.

MARK.   No, this is just what I mean. It's the one easy put-down that's still socially acceptable. Can't put down blacks, can't put down gays, can't put down Jews — that marks you as a racist or a redneck. But men — the one category that's always fair game.

SHELLY.   No, there's one other group.

MARK.   Yeah, what?

SHELLY.   Lawyers.

MARK.   Well, *they* deserve it. Hey, you can't tell me that there's any comparison between men and lawyers. I mean, the idea is insulting.

SHELLY.   Except, of course, a lot of lawyers are men. Most of them, in fact.

MARK.   Coincidence, pure coincidence. You know you've got half of us believing it.

SHELLY.   Half of who?

MARK.   Us.

SHELLY.   People with dicks?

MARK.   Half of us do believe it.

SHELLY.   You've taken a poll?

MARK.   We walk around in a state of constant apology and guilt. "We're sorry, we're sorry — " Like being born a man automatically puts us under a presumption of shmuckiness. "What do you expect from him? He's just a man after all. Doesn't know any better."

SHELLY.   Mark, stop now. Please. *(A beat.)*

MARK.   All right. But —

SHELLY.   "All right, but?"

MARK.   I'm just suggesting it would be a little bit easier — if we're going to stay —

SHELLY.   You said you wanted to stay.

MARK.   I do want to stay. We're going to stay. But I would appreciate it if you didn't help her get out her anger at men in general by beating up on me in particular. I'm not the one who dumped her, if that indeed is what has happened.

SHELLY.   All right, yes. I'll try.

MARK.   Thank you.

SHELLY.   It's just I'm at kind of a loss. What to say to her, what to do.

MARK.   If you hadn't introduced them to begin with —

SHELLY.   Excuse me?

MARK. Jill and Russ. If you hadn't tried to be the match-maker —

SHELLY. I should have known better?

MARK. Well —

SHELLY. I should have foreseen — ?

MARK. Why not?

SHELLY. I don't see how —

MARK. The probability anyway.

SHELLY. That this would happen? How on earth could I have foreseen that this would happen?

MARK. Well, it does a lot doesn't it? More often than not? People don't work out. People fall apart.

SHELLY. So because people mostly don't work, I shouldn't have introduced them?

MARK. Then she wouldn't look at us like it's our fault.

SHELLY. I didn't tell them to get married. I just thought they might show each other a good time.

MARK. Yeah, but even that phrase — "a good time."

SHELLY. What?

MARK. It implies, you know, something that will come to an end. A finite period. Why were you so eager?

SHELLY. Are you asking me to defend myself for trying to make people happy?

MARK. You can't make people happy.

SHELLY. Why not? You make me happy. Usually, generally.

MARK. I don't. I do things. I have good intentions. I try to be considerate and so forth and make choices. The fact is you could be happy or not. You *choose* to be happy. If you wanted to be *not* happy, the same things I do could just as easily piss you off royally. You could go to some support group or something and tell awful stories of how I did the exact same things and they would mostly go, "How do you stand it? Leave the creep."

SHELLY. Well, I'm not going to do that.

MARK. No?

SHELLY. Because I choose to be happy with you.

MARK. Is that true?

SHELLY. Yes.

23

MARK. You're not just being clever?

SHELLY. I don't *be* that kind of clever.

MARK. Wait a second: you're telling me we're happily married?

SHELLY. Yes.

MARK. Wow.

SHELLY. Yes. *(A beat.)*

MARK. You want to go upstairs?

SHELLY. We can't do that either.

MARK. Really?

SHELLY. No. Not yet.

MARK. She's on the phone.

SHELLY. Yeah, but she could get off the phone at any time. She *would* get off the phone. If we went upstairs, she *would* get off the phone. And then she'd look for us. Maybe tap at our door. "You guys busy?"

MARK. That's true. *(Jill enters during the following.)*

SHELLY. Later.

JILL. What later?

SHELLY. I'm going to rub his back.

JILL. Mmmm. Some fun, hunh?

SHELLY. What?

JILL. Just what you were looking forward to, yes? Part of me thinks maybe I should leave —

SHELLY. No. And do what?

JILL. Just because my life has turned to puke, why should I junk up your week?

MARK. Hey, are we complaining?

JILL. Not to my face.

SHELLY. We don't want you to go.

JILL. That's the problem. I don't think I *can* go.

MARK. Of course you can't.

JILL. No, I'm talking about reasons of practicality. If Russ magically suddenly does decide to appear. If I've misread him.

SHELLY. Your phone calls?

JILL. Nothing. Nobody knows where he is, or if they do, they're not telling me. And I understand that. I do. They're his friends mostly. Higher loyalties. Shared histories. If *I* were

24

hiding out with *you,* and I asked you not to tell him I was here if he called, I'm sure you'd respect that. Gee, what do you think? Do you think I sound rational? Do you think I sound fair and reasonable and understanding?

MARK.   Completely. *(Jill picks up Mark's paperback.)*

JILL.   Are you actually reading this?

MARK.   Yes, I believe I am. *(She puts it down.)*

JILL.   What we should do, probably, is rent a video. Something awful. Something we can mock. You ever see *Return to Peyton Place?*

MARK.   No.

JILL.   It was on one of the cable channels. Russ and I watched it. All these incredible archaic Nineteen-fifties values topped off with Fifties hair and paperback versions of Freud. So-and-so's shocking secret. The scandal that rocked a town.

MARK.   Which was?

JILL.   Probably somebody slept with somebody they weren't supposed to. Isn't that what it always is? Actually, it's almost quaint. Looking at what was supposed to be shocking, daring. Kind of a nostalgia rush. Like Jane Russell's boobs in that Western.

MARK.   *The Outlaw.*

JILL.   *(To Shelly.)* Trust a man to remember that, hunh? *(Mark looks at Shelly pointedly. Jill doesn't notice.)* Sometimes I think — you know, to go back to a world where Jane Russell's cleavage was shocking. Who could be shocked by that today, right? Hell, you see more boobs today in *Disney* movies. Jessica Rabbit.

MARK.   I read someplace that he was an ass man.

JILL.   Who?

MARK.   Disney. That if you look at a lot of the cartoons, you'll see that there's a lot of fanny patting.

JILL.   Are you saying Disney had a secret lust for Minnie Mouse?

MARK.   Of course, that's exactly what I'm saying.

JILL.   Then what *are* you saying?

MARK.   Just thought I'd toss in a little ancillary trivia.

JILL.   That Disney was an ass man.

MARK. That's what I read. Or heard.

JILL. What does this have to do with what we were discussing?

MARK. Were we discussing something? Something in particular?

JILL. I thought we were. I was making a point, and I don't usually make points if I'm not discussing something. But then you jump in with that Jane Russell thing —

MARK. I didn't bring up Jane Russell. You brought up Jane Russell.

JILL. You brought up Minnie Mouse's ass.

MARK. I brought up Walt Disney.

JILL. Yeah, why did you do that?

MARK. I'm sorry.

JILL. Well, you should be. What does it matter, really, what Walt Disney was? I mean, he's gone, and he's left behind all these wonderful films, so why do you have to attack him?

MARK. Is that what I was doing?

JILL. You called him an ass man.

MARK. You think that was an attack?

JILL. You think that was a compliment?

MARK. I think it's just a comment. With no particular value attached.

JILL. Sometimes I think it would be nice to put up a fence around people and they would be, like, protected people? No matter what you dug up about them, we don't want to know. Like Disney. I don't want to know. Or that stuff about Errol Flynn maybe being a Nazi spy. Or Joan Crawford and the coat hangers. Or whatever Chaplin was supposed to have done. Leave it alone, you know? Leave it alone. What's going to be helped by learning shitty things about people like that? All it does is make you feel like a fool for having enjoyed their stuff. Like you watch this great comedy and somebody tells you this guy who, even though he's been dead fifty years, is making you laugh — but somebody tells you, "Yeah, but did you know he was a drunk and a child molester and he sent Christmas cards to Hitler?" Spoilsports.

MARK. So you're proposing legislation?

JILL.   Sure, why not? There's the Endangered Species Act, so why not —

MARK.   The Endangered Celebrities Act?

JILL.   Not just celebrities. Martin Luther King. Isn't there a point where the good stuff they've done outweighs the smaller shit?

MARK.   What do you think, Shelly?

SHELLY.   *(Who hasn't been paying attention.)* Hunh?

MARK.   What do you think?

SHELLY.   I guess I agree.

JILL.   What do you agree with?

SHELLY.   That it's a shame that people who've done good things — I mean basically what you said.

MARK.   But here's the problem.

JILL.   OK, let's hear it.

MARK.   Are you saying that people who've done really good things, we should excuse the bad things they do?

JILL.   Where's your problem?

MARK.   Well, someone might get the idea that you can get a free ride on the shit you do if you do a lot of good stuff. I mean, it could be interpreted as a license. "Oh, I cured cancer, so it's OK for me to rob a convenience store." "Oh, she's a great actress so she can bust up anybody else's marriage she wants to."

JILL.   So you're saying you would have given Gandhi a parking ticket.

MARK.   I don't think Gandhi owned a car.

JILL.   I'm talking about the principle —

MARK.   If you're asking me if I think there should be special rules for a certain class of people, no I don't think there should be special rules. I don't think being a celebrity should protect someone from the consequences of behaving badly.

JILL.   No, see, this is what you don't get. I'm not talking about them. I'm not talking about protecting *them*. I'm talking about protecting *us*.

MARK.   What from?

SHELLY.   Disillusion.

JILL.   See? She gets it. Your wife gets it. Sometimes the heart only can take so much. You don't want more bad news. Especially unnecessary bad news. Stuff that you can't change. I can't change that Errol Flynn was a Nazi spy, if he was. But knowing that changes me. It makes me not be able to enjoy *Robin Hood*. And I'd rather enjoy *Robin Hood* than know something I can't change.

MARK.   You'd rather not know.

JILL.   I'd rather not know.

MARK.   So why have you been on the phone the past hour and a half?

SHELLY.   Mark. *(A beat.)*

JILL.   Thank you. That was cute.

MARK.   I shouldn't have said that.

JILL.   It's not the same thing.

MARK.   No, it isn't.

JILL.   Russ isn't a celebrity.

MARK.   No. What I said was dumb. I apologize. *(A beat.)*

SHELLY.   You said something about renting a video. Is that what you'd like to do?

JILL.   I don't know. That sound like fun to you?

SHELLY.   Could be OK.

JILL.   Where would I go around here?

SHELLY.   I think there's a video joint on the main drag. What do you say I go with you?

JILL.   No, I'd like to do this by myself. I don't want another opinion in there, because I really intend to rent something terrible.

SHELLY.   You'd feel inhibited?

JILL.   Yeah. Maybe a monster movie.

SHELLY.   OK, but not one of the new ones with the really convincing gore. One of the old ones from the Fifties.

JILL.   Vincent Price.

SHELLY.   I haven't seen one of those in years.

JILL.   *(To Mark.)* And if you know something nasty about Vincent Price, I don't want to hear it.

MARK.   I hear he was a gentleman and a humanitarian.

JILL.   Good. And I could get some microwave popcorn. Does that idea appeal?

SHELLY.   Sounds good to me.

JILL.   I feel pathetic.

SHELLY.   You aren't.

JILL.   Good, I'm reassured. Oh, Christ. *(Jill begins to cry. Shelly holds her as Mark stays put. A beat.)*

MARK.   There, there. *(Shelly shoots him a look. Mark shrugs. Fade out.)*

SCENE THREE

Night. Moonlight. Jill enters from around the house, leading Glen, a casually dressed man in his mid-forties, to the deck. She signals that he should have a seat, puts down her purse, then goes inside the house. Glen, a little ill-at-ease, looks around a little. Lights suddenly illuminate the deck, and Jill emerges with wine glasses and a bottle of wine.

JILL.   A little light on the subject.

GLEN.   Hi.

JILL.   This is better, don't you think? At least we'll be able to hear each other.

GLEN.   Ernie's usually isn't that noisy.

JILL.   "Usually" being when weekend visitors aren't infesting the place?

GLEN.   You aren't going to hear me complain about weekenders. Half the businesses in the area would probably go under if it weren't for them.

JILL.   But it would be nice if they hadn't discovered Ernie's?

GLEN.   Ernie isn't complaining. *(Smiles at her shyly.)* And I'm not complaining tonight.

JILL.   Wine?

GLEN.   Sure. *(She pours some for both of them. They drink. The sound of a couple's laughter from some distance. Glen looks in the direction of where it came from.)* Looks like a couple of your neighbors are having a midnight frolic.

JILL.   Where?

GLEN.   *(Pointing.)* Over there, see?

JILL.   *(Laughing.)* Oh yes.

GLEN.   Wonder where the expression came from? The "dipping" part I understand. But the "skinny"? That there is what I call "middle-age-spread-dipping." *(Laughs. Slaps his stomach.)* Like I should talk, right?

JILL.   Well, they're having fun. Midnight splash. What the hell.

GLEN.   I was in Los Angeles once, stayed with the older brother of a friend of mine. He was an engineer at A&M Records. Real heady stuff for a kid. Which I was then. This guy — the brother — had actually been in the same studio with Sergio Mendes! Can you imagine?

JILL.   Cool, man.

GLEN.   Must have been the early seventies. Anyway, one night he has some friends over. Including some ladies. He had a pool —

JILL.   I think I see where this is going.

GLEN.   Well, I was still young, shy.

JILL.   So you didn't?

GLEN.   No actually, I did.

JILL.   Your basic birthday suit?

GLEN.   God, talk about self-conscious. But the thing is, when I took my glasses off — I'm real near-sighted —

JILL.   *(He's not wearing glasses.)* Contacts?

GLEN.   Uh, yeah. But I couldn't see much of anything. Everything was a blur. And because everything was a blur for me, on some level I kind of believed —

JILL.   — everything was a blur for them, too?

GLEN.   If I couldn't see them, how could they see me?

JILL.   Logical.

GLEN.   I thought so.

JILL.   Had a good time, hunh?

GLEN.   It was fun.

JILL.   You were how old? A kid you said.

GLEN.   Early twenties.

JILL.   You even remember her name?

GLEN.   Whose name?

JILL.   Whoever she was you ended up with.

GLEN.   No, that didn't happen.

JILL.   No? All that potential for nookie and nothing? That's all there is to the story? Just that you paddled around bare-assed in the same pool with some women you couldn't see very well?

GLEN.   It wasn't only women. But yeah, that was it.

JILL.   But this was the early seventies, right? Los Angeles.

Drugs, presumably.

GLEN. Some pot.

JILL. All that stuff working for you and all you did was the backstroke? That's what you call a good time?

GLEN. Actually, there was something nice about being able to all be naked together without feeling the necessity of taking it further. It's like a truce had been declared.

JILL. A truce? From what?

GLEN. The usual will-we-won't-we stuff. Not that anybody said anything like that. Made an announcement or anything. Just there was a sort of understanding.

JILL. A sex-free zone?

GLEN. Hunh?

JILL. Like a nuclear-free zone, a sex-free zone.

GLEN. Like that, yeah. No pressure. No expectations. We all felt safe. Like we were all observing, well, like I said — a flag of truce.

JILL. I'd like to know where to get one of those.

GLEN. A flag of truce?

JILL. Sometimes to be able to call a time out. To be able to say, "Hey, could we, for a little while, put all this crap aside?"

GLEN. You know *The Left Hand of Darkness*?

JILL. No, what's that?

GLEN. Science fiction novel? Ursula LeGuin?

JILL. I'm not into science fiction. I don't mean that in a snobby way. It's just I haven't read anything later than H.G. Wells.

GLEN. Anyway, she wrote this book that's set on this alien world where there's only one sex.

JILL. One sex like it's the planet of the Amazons?

GLEN. No, it's more — well, they're not exactly hermaphrodites —

JILL. How do these aliens do it, reproduce? Or don't they?

GLEN. They have cycles.

JILL. Cycles?

GLEN. I'm not explaining this right.

JILL. No, cycles how, cycles how?

GLEN.   OK, say you're an alien: one part of the cycle you've got male characteristics, the other part you're kind of female.

JILL.   So how does the couple thing work?

GLEN.   Say you're in an alien relationship — when you're sort of the man, your significant alien other is sort of the woman. A month or two later, it's the other way around.

JILL.   Oh, so you take turns having periods. I like that idea.

GLEN.   I don't remember the details of the story all that clearly, but I think the point of the book is, if everyone's male sometimes and female sometimes, what changes does this make in the society?

JILL.   Probably, you know what, there'd be couples who would be perpetually out of synch — when one's a guy the other's a guy, when one's a woman — right?

GLEN.   Sure, star-crossed lovers.

JILL.   Though, see, with *my* luck, I'd be the one person in this alien world who had some kind of glandular condition and I'd get trapped somewhere in the cycle, *jammed* — end up combining the worst aspects of both sexes.

GLEN.   Oh?

JILL.   I'd probably still be stuck with childbirth, *and* I'd be an asshole.

GLEN.   The divorce was pretty recent, hunh?

JILL.   You can tell?

GLEN.   It takes one to know one.

JILL.   You, too?

GLEN.   Yup.

JILL.   That was your ex, wasn't it?

GLEN.   What was?

JILL.   You were yelling at on the phone? At Ernie's?

GLEN.   Was I yelling?

JILL.   Maybe you were just trying to be heard over the crowd.

GLEN.   That was probably it. It can get awfully noisy at Ernie's.

JILL.   Particularly with us weekenders.

GLEN.   I'm not complaining.

JILL.   But I'm right? About who you were on the phone with?

GLEN.   How'd you guess?

JILL.   I heard the word "visitation."

GLEN.   That's what I was supposed to be doing tonight.

JILL.   Seeing your kid? Or is it kids?

GLEN.   Kid. Son. Darryl.

JILL.   So what went wrong?

GLEN.   Well, I was running late, so I stopped by Ernie's to use the phone, to call and say that. But that I was on my way. And she says —

JILL.   Your ex?

GLEN.   — she says, "On your way to what? He's not here." I say, "What do you mean, it's my weekend." She says it isn't and she'll check the calendar. And when she does, it turns out it *is* my weekend, but he's away on a sleepover so it'll have to be next weekend I see him. I say I'm busy next weekend. She says something about what it means if I'm too busy to see my son, and so on and so on.

JILL.   And that's when you tried to be heard over the crowd.

GLEN.   You weekenders are a noisy bunch.

JILL.   Sorry about that.

GLEN.   But that's how I ended up at Ernie's. *(Referring to the skinny-dippers.)* Oh look, they're going in.

JILL.   He could afford to cut back on those donuts. You like it around here?

GLEN.   Oh yeah, this is nice.

JILL.   No, I don't mean here, I mean *around* here.

GLEN.   You mean to live?

JILL.   The city's beginning to get to me. Maybe it's time for me to —

GLEN.   I could clear out a corner in my trailer.

JILL.   You actually live in a trailer?

GLEN.   That's me, trailer trash.

JILL.   City's for youngsters. For women it is anyway. Girls. When I was in my twenties, I'd go to a party, I'd know it was my option.

GLEN.   What was?

JILL.   If something was going to happen. I used to be pretty hot.

GLEN.   What do you mean "used to be?"

JILL. A man would come up to me and I had this smile I would turn on. No, not turn on. Turn up.

GLEN. Turn up?

JILL. Like it was on a dimmer switch. Tease it up so it kinda flickered around the edges of my lips.

GLEN. And that smile said what?

JILL. "Tell me why I should care. Why you're worth it."

GLEN. You were a heartbreaker.

JILL. I was cruel. I really was. But you can't get away with being cruel when you're pushing forty. Unless you have money. Then you can hire people to be cruel to. I don't have money. Not *that* kind of money. In case you were wondering.

GLEN. Hey, I'm out of here.

JILL. Men fifteen years ago I wouldn't have looked twice at, probably would have cut short —

GLEN. Back in your cruel days?

JILL. All of a sudden these men — with the thinning hair and the tummies creeping over the belts — they're the ones with the goods. And dames like me — we're a glut on the market.

GLEN. Don't talk like that.

JILL. No, I have a healthy opinion of myself. A healthy appreciation of my gifts. But the city is lousy with gifted ladies of a certain age. Straight, single guys, on the other hand —

GLEN. A rare commodity?

JILL. Sometimes I look around, try to find someone to fix up some of my divorced girlfriends with. Something even vaguely suitable. And I'd think, thank God I'm not one of them. How lucky I am. Was. *(Beat.)* You'd make out like crazy in the city.

GLEN. Is that so?

JILL. No, you really would. Straight, presentable, charming —

GLEN. Thank you.

JILL. I'm not kidding. Clean you up, put you in a decent jacket, you could write your own ticket. You've got talent, kid.

GLEN. Tell you what, you can be my personal manager.

JILL. Maybe I'll take you up on that.

GLEN.   I thought you were going to move up here.

JILL.   Into your trailer. That's right.

GLEN.   Well, give me a few years. Maybe I'll give the city a shot.

JILL.   Why the wait?

GLEN.   Darryl.

JILL.   Your son.

GLEN.   Got to be around for my kid. If he needs to call me. His mother's crazy, you know.

JILL.   I think so.

GLEN.   Not a bad person exactly, but her wheel's definitely slipping off the axle. He needs to know he's got one parent he can depend on. Till he takes off for college anyway.

JILL.   What's that — four years? Five?

GLEN.   About.

JILL.   You let me know when. Course, I reserve the right of first refusal. Kidding. What do you do anyway? You a teacher? You talk like a teacher.

GLEN.   I've done some different things. These days, I'm mostly a carpenter. Cabinet work. Building decks like this one.

JILL.   And how *is* this deck? Your professional opinion.

GLEN.   Good job.

JILL.   I work with carpenters sometimes.

GLEN.   Really, how?

JILL.   If I need something built for a function.

GLEN.   A function? What do you —

JILL.   I'm a partner at Iris Broder Promotions.

GLEN.   And that is — ?

JILL.   Events planning.

GLEN.   And that is — ?

JILL.   Say you've got a daughter's getting married and five, six hundred grand to do it up right.

GLEN.   Five, six hundred grand?

JILL.   Hey, I know one topped a million two.

GLEN.   So you do what?

JILL.   Conceptualize, organize, schedule. If we're doing something on a gypsy theme, maybe I'll fly violinists in from Budapest. Or if I need a gazebo to be built in the ballroom

36

at the Plaza, I'll work with designers. Keep an eye on construction.

GLEN.   Carpenters.

JILL.   And electricians, yeah. Though I don't really deal directly at that level. That's for the person I've brought in to supervise to handle. And then, you know, photographers. Sometimes it's on a level where there's press to deal with.

GLEN.   Are there enough weddings to make a living at this?

JILL.   Not just weddings. Benefits. *Some*body has to plan Carnegie Hall's hundredth birthday. These things don't take care of themselves. *Some*body has to plan when Queen Elizabeth comes to visit.

GLEN.   And you're that somebody?

JILL.   Well, not those particular gigs, but stuff like that. It's like being a producer.

GLEN.   A lot of people work on these things, hunh?

JILL.   For the big projects, it can go north of a hundred.

GLEN.   And you're the boss.

JILL.   Oh, I don't know.

GLEN.   You said you hire people —

JILL.   Some.

GLEN.   And you can fire them.

JILL.   Yeah.

GLEN.   *(His case is made.)* You're the boss.

JILL.   I'm *a* boss.

GLEN.   *Do* you fire people?

JILL.   I try to hire the right people to begin with so I don't have to.

GLEN.   But you *have* fired people?

JILL.   Part of the job.

GLEN.   You set standards, and if people don't meet them —

JILL.   First, maybe a warning shot over their head.

GLEN.   A touch of the whip?

JILL.   Just to get them focussed. Mostly it works.

GLEN.   But sometimes — *(He signals, "Out of there.")*

JILL.   Part of the job.

GLEN.   And if you fire them from one job, you're not likely to hire them for another.

JILL.   No.

GLEN.   So when you're in the neighborhood, people are on their best behavior.

JILL.   Yes, I inspire fear. No, I'm pretty easy to get along with. Long as you do your job.

GLEN.   I'll remember that.

JILL.   Doing this kind of work can spoil you. You make a decision, you tell people the way you want it —

GLEN.   They do it.

JILL.   But outside of work — People have this annoying tendency to do what *they* want to do.

GLEN.   And you can't fire them.

JILL.   There are days I'd like to. Like my mother. She'd open an envelope from me, there's this pink slip, maybe a little handwritten note. "Thanks for all your hard work, but we're downsizing the family. Best of luck in your future parenting career."

GLEN.   Well, I don't know what you'd do up here.

JILL.   No?

GLEN.   I don't guess there's much money to be made planning events in these parts. Unless you wanted to organize the wet T-shirt competition at Ernie's.

JILL.   I don't think I'm qualified.

GLEN.   Well, you could pick up some bucks if you *won* the wet T-shirt competition.

JILL.   I don't think I'm qualified.

GLEN.   So what brought you to Ernie's anyway?

JILL.   Well, I went out to rent a video. But Friday night, the pickings are pretty thin. There I was, holding *The Mighty Ducks* in one hand and *Porky's III* in the other, seriously debating which was the better choice — Then I saw Ernie's through the window.

GLEN.   So if the video selection had been better, you and I wouldn't have met.

JILL.   Talk about fate.

GLEN.   And I was right? The divorce is pretty recent?

JILL.   So recent it hasn't happened yet. Part of the reason I'm here actually. Visiting with friends.

GLEN. That's who *you* called from the bar.

JILL. Didn't want them to worry about me. They're nice people.

GLEN. They have names?

JILL. Mark and Shelly. I knew Mark back in college. Actually, we lived together for a couple years after. Mark and I.

GLEN. What broke you up?

JILL. We were awfully young. Too young to be thinking about permanent. So, yeah, we broke up, thinking that maybe someday, after we had enough mileage, we'd check each other out again. And a year or two later — surprise, surprise — he met Shelly and they got married. And, you know, I wanted to dislike her. I really did. But somehow I couldn't manage it.

GLEN. You all ended up being friends?

JILL. Isn't that nauseating? Actually, she's the one who introduced me to Russell. My husband. My soon-to-be-ex-husband.

GLEN. Breaking up's a bitch. *(A beat.)* Sometimes when I'm on the phone with her, just the sound of her voice —

JILL. Oh, yeah, right —

GLEN. For years, that was programmed into me. "That's the voice of the person I love."

JILL. Conditioned response?

GLEN. The sound triggers this wave of feeling —

JILL. Must be what ex-Catholics go through when they hear organ music.

GLEN. And then, right after that first wave of, "Oh, she's the person I love," there's a second wave —

JILL. That says, "Hey, wait a minute."

GLEN. I would really like to know when that goes away. So that when I hear her voice, it's just another voice.

JILL. Do you think that ever happens?

GLEN. I sure hope it will. I've noticed it's changed the way I answer the phone.

JILL. How did you used to answer the phone?

GLEN. *(Lightly.)* Hello?

JILL. And now?

GLEN. *(Neutrally.)* Hello?

JILL.   And that's why?

GLEN.   Well, it could be her. Don't want to answer *(Lightly.)* "Hello?" if it's her.

JILL.   You afraid that she'll think that you're happy?

GLEN.   I say it that way and it's her, I have to do a whole readjustment thing.

JILL.   *(Darkly.)* What — "Oh, it's you?"

GLEN.   Like in music, a modulation to a different key.

JILL.   Major to minor?

GLEN.   I do the modulation too abruptly, she gets offended and pissed off. So I do this more neutral "hello."

JILL.   This leaves you positioned to modulate to whatever key you want.

GLEN.   Maximum flexibility.

JILL.   So it's like the doorbell rings, and you're looking through the peep-hole first.

GLEN.   Well, we're grownups now. You can't be a grownup and automatically assume that whatever comes over the phone is going to be good news.

JILL.   Is that what being a grownup means? Living in the expectation that you could be whacked at any time?

GLEN.   Yeah. But there's some good stuff, too. Being able to stay up as late as you want. Not having to take phys ed. Not having to eat beets.

JILL.   Not to mention the right to vote.

GLEN.   Well, I can't do that anymore.

JILL.   "Can't?" What did you do? Hold up a filling station?

GLEN.   No, a bank actually. *(She laughs.)* No, really.

JILL.   You held up an actual bank?

GLEN.   Over in Spring Hill, one town over that way.

JILL.   You're serious.

GLEN.   Unh-hunh.

JILL.   Wow.

GLEN.   I used to do a little coaching for the high school track team.

JILL.   What does that have to do with —

GLEN.   Well, I was on the way to a practice session. I stopped in at the Spring Hill branch of my bank to pick up some cash.

I'm standing on line, and I put my hand in my pocket and realize I have a starter's pistol with me.

JILL. So the idea just popped into your head.

GLEN. I get the money, no problem. I jump in my car and I'm driving away and I go about two blocks and I stop. And I think, "Did I just do what I think I did?" And I look down at the seat next to me and there's this money there. "Yeah, I guess I did."

JILL. "Oh shit?"

GLEN. So I get out of the car and I flag down a cop. What do I want, he asks me. I tell him that I've just done something I think he'd find of interest.

JILL. He must have gotten a kick out of that.

GLEN. Made his day. Made my year. Actually more like six months with good behavior. My behavior was very good. I was a model prisoner. The warden said so himself.

JILL. They put you away?

GLEN. Yes, they did.

JILL. But didn't they understand you'd flipped out?

GLEN. That's why it was only six months. Armed robbery charge, I could have still been in there. I think I got a pretty good deal, actually.

JILL. Why'd you do it? Do you know?

GLEN. Well, some of it was money, obviously. The divorce was getting under way and that wasn't cheap. But I thought about it a lot afterwards — I had six months *to* think about it — and I think it was that so much of my life was stuff that was happening *to* me. Just me reacting to whatever garbage was being fired my way. A sustained defensive posture. And for a second there, with that pistol in my hand, I had the illusion that *I* was setting the agenda for once. What I did might have been stupid — *was* stupid — but it was an action I was taking.

JILL. Your choice to *be* stupid.

GLEN. Funny thing, my son —

JILL. Darryl?

GLEN. It's about the only thing he's shown me any respect for.

JILL.   Holding up a bank?

GLEN.   He's thirteen. Here. *(He reaches for his wallet.)*

JILL.   Picture time?

GLEN.   Sorry if it's corny.

JILL.   No, no, it's nice corny. Let's see — *(She looks.)* Yeah, that's a thirteen-year-old boy, all right. He'll grow out of that.

GLEN.   You think?

JILL.   *You* did.

GLEN.   The divorce wasn't my idea.

JILL.   Another guy?

GLEN.   Mmmmm.

JILL.   That must have done wonders for your ego.

GLEN.   Made me stand real tall in my son's eyes. Thirteen years old — you have all of these semi-adult impulses and appetites, but you don't have the power to do anything about them. So you look around for someone to identify with who's got muscle.

JILL.   Sylvester Stallone, Spiderman, Arnold.

GLEN.   You sure don't look at a dad who couldn't hold the family together. That's the first job of a dad, and he thinks I blew it.

JILL.   But robbing the bank —

GLEN.   The most dumb-ass thing I've done in my life, and that's what he gives me points for.

JILL.   Well, you know it's just a matter of time before he grows up and sees you clearly and maturely and learns to hate you for who you really are.

GLEN.   You read about how kids take after their parents? For his sake I hope not.

JILL.   Hey, you want to take a break from beating yourself up?

GLEN.   And do what?

JILL.   Well, I have an idea. *(Over the following, she disappears through the door.)*

GLEN.   Where you going?

JILL.   Hold on. You'll see. *(Slow, romantic music begins from offstage. She returns carrying the boom box it's coming from.)* This should do it.

GLEN. Do what?

JILL. It's called atmosphere.

GLEN. Oh?

JILL. Or did you think I invited you out here to talk about social themes in genre fiction?

GLEN. I'd like to know why.

JILL. Why what?

GLEN. Me. Why me?

JILL. Are you complaining?

GLEN. No, not at all. But it would be nice if I could believe there was something about me in particular —

JILL. Well, that goes without saying.

GLEN. My eyes.

JILL. Yeah, that's it.

GLEN. It's one of my better features, my eyes.

JILL. That's what did it for me. I got the feeling there's all kinds of stuff going on behind there.

GLEN. You're very perceptive, you know that?

JILL. So I was right?

GLEN. Oh yeah, there's lots of stuff going on behind there.

JILL. Well sure. I'm not into, you know —

GLEN. Meaningless, anonymous sex?

JILL. Sure. It's too dangerous.

GLEN. If you had known I was a bank robber?

JILL. Well, it's not like you do it all the time. It's not like that's your vocation.

GLEN. No. Strictly amateur standing. I should tell you something.

JILL. What?

GLEN. I really haven't been with anybody else since my wife and I broke up. The divorce.

JILL. Me neither.

GLEN. Oh, well then you understand.

JILL. We can take it real easy, if that's what you want.

GLEN. It's not that I'm made out of china.

JILL. No, I do understand. But while we're talking, if there's something you used to do with her — with your wife — in bed, you know?

43

GLEN.   Like what?

JILL.   Oh, scratch her head or something — like a habit thing — if you could do me the favor of not doing that with me.

GLEN.   OK.

JILL.   Tonight's going to be whatever it's going to be, but I would like it if it's me you're with, not that I'm a stand-in. Or a lie-in.

GLEN.   You got it.

JILL.   All right then.

GLEN.   Shall my lawyer call your lawyer, draw up the contract?

JILL.   Hunh?

GLEN.   A joke.

JILL.   I don't understand it.

GLEN.   We've just gone through this negotiation.

JILL.   *(Laughs.)* Oh. Yes.

GLEN.   I mean, we've basically decided what we're going to do and we haven't even touched each other.

JILL.   We should get around to that.

GLEN.   Break the ice a little.

JILL.   Every journey begins with one step. *(A beat. Glen goes to her and kisses her.)*

GLEN.   Hello.

JILL.   Hello.

GLEN.   This could work.

JILL.   For tonight anyway. *(She kisses him, then leads him into a dance. The door opens and Mark enters.)*

MARK.   Jill —

JILL.   Mark. I thought you guys were asleep.

MARK.   Well, no.

JILL.   We didn't wake you?

MARK.   No. *(Jill turns off the tape player.)*

JILL.   Glen, this is Mark. One of the friends I was telling you about.

GLEN.   Hello.

JILL.   Where's Shelly?

MARK.   Up in our room.

44

JILL. (To Glen.) Shelly is Mark's wife.

GLEN. That's right.

MARK. Jill, could I have a word with you for a second?

JILL. What kind of word?

MARK. Something to discuss.

GLEN. Why don't I hit the john?

MARK. Good idea. Inside and to the right.

GLEN. Got you. (Glen exits into the house. Jill and Mark look at each other for a second.)

JILL. What?

MARK. Do I need to say it?

JILL. You don't approve.

MARK. This is a mistake, Jill.

JILL. I'm very grateful for your assessment.

MARK. Not just my assessment.

JILL. Shelly's too?

MARK. You know it's the wrong thing to do.

JILL. You can see deep in my heart, hunh? You can tell this?

MARK. I don't need to see deep in your heart to know.

JILL. Mark, you're about to embarrass yourself.

MARK. I don't think so.

JILL. Mark, this is not a subject on which you are entitled to offer an opinion. Not one I have to take seriously anyway.

MARK. Look, I understand what's going on here. You're angry, you're hurt. Russ has behaved badly, but that doesn't mean it's a good idea for you to —

JILL. I thought you didn't like Russ —

MARK. I like Russ OK.

JILL. (Continuing.) — so what are you doing, acting like a human chastity belt for him?

MARK. I'm not doing anything "for" him —

JILL. Is this you keeping faith with the code?

MARK. Code? What code?

JILL. One guy to another.

MARK. Oh, for Christ's sake —

JILL. Like you're bound to act as his stand-in?

MARK. This has nothing to do with him —

JILL. Then why are you getting involved?

MARK. — it has to do with you.

JILL. What you think's best for me.

MARK. Yes.

JILL. Thank you. I'm touched. Butt out.

MARK. Jill —

JILL. You've proven how concerned you are about me.

MARK. What does that mean?

JILL. Think about it.

MARK. Let's not dig up ancient bullshit.

JILL. That's how you characterize it.

MARK. What's going on is not about what happened between you and me a hundred million years ago —

JILL. Oh, it's up to *you* what this is about?

MARK. What's going on is right here and now. This guy you've picked up.

JILL. How do you know he isn't an old friend I happened to meet?

MARK. He isn't.

JILL. How do you know?

MARK. He's not an old friend. You met him in a bar.

JILL. How do you know? Were you listening in?

MARK. It's obvious.

JILL. How?

MARK. I'm not blind.

JILL. Right now I wish you were. Blind and deaf.

MARK. Jill —

JILL. Not to mention mute.

MARK. You pick this guy up, you tell him a lot of lies —

JILL. What lies?

MARK. How you're almost divorced. That we suggested you come up to console you.

JILL. How would you like it if I put a glass to the wall and listened in on you and Shelly?

MARK. It wasn't a matter of putting a glass to the wall. That's our window up there.

JILL. And you couldn't close it out of respect for my privacy?

MARK. Jill, we're friends. This guy can't be important enough for you to risk screwing up our friendship.

JILL.   Then why did you come out here, if he isn't that important?

MARK.   I don't want to see you get —

JILL.   Hurt? Is that what you were going to say?

MARK.   All right, if you don't give a damn about yourself, then how about us?

JILL.   What's it your concern? It isn't you he's going to sleep with.

MARK.   Maybe Shelly and I don't want a stranger under our roof.

JILL.   What do you mean your roof? You put up half for the week. Does putting up half make it yours?

MARK.   We put up half under the assumption of what this week would be.

JILL.   Yeah, well it isn't. So does that give you veto power?

MARK.   It's Russ's money, too. He wouldn't approve of you doing this.

JILL.   Russ no longer has power of approval. He gave that up when he defaulted this week. Anyway, he's probably out there boffing some bimbo even as we speak.

MARK.   Well, if he is, that doesn't make it right.

JILL.   Of course it doesn't make it right, but how is that relevant? The question is whether you and Shelly have the authority to tell me what I can do. You are not my parents or my legal guardians, so I submit you have no such authority.

MARK.   You don't think we have any rights in this?

JILL.   Not as regards my behavior.

MARK.   You don't think Shelly and I have the right not to share an intimate environment with some guy we don't know much less trust?

JILL.   Then lock your door.

MARK.   That's no answer.

JILL.   I don't owe you an answer. You've turned into a such a smug, arrogant, self-righteous jerk —

MARK.   Call me names if you want to —

JILL.   And I don't need your permission to call you names, thank you.

MARK. He's not staying here.

JILL. And how are you going to enforce that? You going to throw him out? Physically?

MARK. I will do what I have to.

JILL. Just a little clue to you, as a friend — you don't have the equipment to carry off the macho pose.

MARK. Is this what it all comes down to? You taking cheap shots at me?

JILL. Disillusioning, ain't it?

MARK. Jill, please.

JILL. Fuck off, Mark. *(The sound of a car engine turning over.)* What's that? *(She runs around the side of the house, calling —)* Glen! Glen! Come back here! You dickless bastard! *(The sound of the car driving away. Mark picks up her purse, takes out her keys. Hearing her returning, he puts the purse down in a place different than where he found it. She re-enters, notices the purse is in a different place. She looks at him suspiciously.)* Were you in my purse? *(She looks in her purse. She looks up at Mark.)* OK, hand them over.

MARK. Jill —

JILL. Give them to me now.

MARK. Don't you think you ought to — *(Jill suddenly socks him one, knocking him on his ass. His hand flies open and the keys fall onto the deck. Jill scoops them up and runs off the deck and disappears offstage. The sound of her car starting and driving away. Mark, a little stunned, gets up as Shelly emerges.)*

SHELLY. What?

MARK. Jesus, what a punch.

SHELLY. He hit you?

MARK. No, *she* did. She wanted her keys. Her car keys.

SHELLY. What about him? The guy?

MARK. He took off, drove away. Said he was going in to use the john and slipped out the front door. I think maybe he heard what was going on between Jill and me.

SHELLY. Wouldn't be surprised. I heard it and I was upstairs.

MARK. That's what she wanted her car keys for.

SHELLY. To chase after him?

MARK.   I guess. I don't know. I can't believe it — she hit me. I haven't been hit since Gus Teddis nearly broke my nose in high school.

SHELLY.   You aren't going to hold that against her.

MARK.   Why not?

SHELLY.   She's upset.

MARK.   What if I got upset and walloped her?

SHELLY.   That would be different.

MARK.   Because I'm a guy? It's OK to punch out guys?

SHELLY.   OK, come on, enough.

MARK.   You think this is funny, don't you?

SHELLY.   No, I don't. Do you want some help?

MARK.   I don't need help.

SHELLY.   Hey, I'm sorry.

MARK.   Let's just go to bed, OK? Let's just get some sleep.

SHELLY.   OK. Let me just pick up —

MARK.   Don't pick up after her. It's her mess, she should pick up after herself.

SHELLY.   Yes, but it's our stuff. Our glasses. *(A beat.)*

MARK.   Do what you want. I don't care. *(He exits leaving Shelly alone on the deck. She hesitates for a second, then picks up the glasses and the boom box and exits into the house.)*

SCENE FOUR

The next morning. Shelly is sitting on the deck, reading. Jill enters from around the side of the house. She doesn't step onto the deck, but leans against the railing.

SHELLY.   Hello, slugger.

JILL.   Where's Mark?

SHELLY.   In the shower.

JILL.   How pissed is he?

SHELLY.   On what scale of measurement?

JILL.   Well, what would I have to do to get back into his good graces? A simple apology? Abject grovelling? A blowjob?

SHELLY.   I don't think a blowjob would do it.

JILL.   Funny, it always used to.

SHELLY.   Well, then you'd be stuck with the problem of getting back into *my* good graces. Or does that matter to you?

JILL.   Of course it matters.

SHELLY.   Is that so?

JILL.   What makes you say —

SHELLY.   *(Interrupting.)* Did you think that I would applaud your belting my husband? Did you think that this would endear you to me?

JILL.   Sorry. I didn't mean to intrude on *your* prerogatives.

SHELLY.   That's another joke, right?

JILL.   Oh, lighten up. I didn't maim the guy. In a moment of anger — and I think with some justification — I took a little swing at him.

SHELLY.   That little swing has produced a very colorful eye.

JILL.   Well, I was frustrated.

SHELLY.   If being frustrated justified taking swings at someone, you'd be in a wheelchair now.

JILL.   Really?

SHELLY.   You're not the easiest houseguest.

JILL.   Excuse me, I paid my share for this week. I am your

house*mate*. Not a guest.

SHELLY.   All right, then don't make us treat you like one.

JILL.   I'm not.

SHELLY.   We came here to relax, not to look after —

JILL.   *(Over.)* Have I asked you to look after me?

SHELLY.   Not in so many words.

JILL.   Not in any words at all. Your company, your support, that's appreciated, but —

SHELLY.   *(Over.)* We see what you're going through — You're someone we care about.

JILL.   So of course this deep wellspring of compassion licenses you to act like cops?

SHELLY.   We're not doing that.

JILL.   *(Over.)* Mark took my keys. Out of my purse. My car keys. Went into my purse when my back was turned and confiscated them. Like he was the fucking highway patrol and I was a drunk. Or do you think that was right?

SHELLY.   I'm not saying it was.

JILL.   Or do you let him prowl through *your* purse?

SHELLY.   Point taken.

JILL.   Not to mention sticking his nose into my personal choices. Holding my keys hostage to deny me the *possibility* of choice. I asked him to give them back. He refused. What was I supposed to do?

SHELLY.   No, I'm surprised you were so restrained. Especially when chairs were handy and you could have bashed him over the head.

JILL.   That would have been excessive. That orange juice looks good.

SHELLY.   Help yourself. *(Jill steps onto the deck for the first time in the scene and pours some juice during the following.)*

JILL.   I needed the keys quick if I was going to have any chance of catching up. I needed them.

SHELLY.   And *did* you catch up with — what's his name?

JILL.   *(Drinking.)* Yes. He's a nice guy.

SHELLY.   Funny, last night I remember you yelling something — something about him being a dickless bastard.

JILL.   Well, I was wrong. On both counts.

SHELLY. Unh-hunh.

JILL. It's been a while since somebody made me feel like — since somebody looked at me differently than the way they'd look at — I don't know — a bar of used soap.

SHELLY. Last night you felt like new soap?

JILL. Do you want the graphic details?

SHELLY. Would any of them surprise me?

JILL. It was your basic standard-issue sex, and I make no apologies for enjoying it.

SHELLY. He's a nice guy.

JILL. He *is*.

SHELLY. Even if he is a bank robber.

JILL. He's not really a bank robber. Just —

SHELLY. — someone who robbed a bank.

JILL. Yeah.

SHELLY. There's a difference.

JILL. If you heard the whole story, you know that he just flipped out for a moment.

SHELLY. *He* was frustrated, too, right? He robs a bank, you deck my husband.

JILL. It's not the same —

SHELLY. *(Over.)* No, sounds like you're made for each other.

JILL. It was about consolation. I cried a little on his shoulder, he cried a little on mine.

SHELLY. Another sensitive man.

JILL. It's not like this is the beginning of a great romance. There was no pretending that. We were what each other needed last night. Simple as that.

SHELLY. Then it's lucky you found each other.

JILL. I mean, come on, are you going to tell me you never in your life had a nice therapeutic fuck? I understand what's going on here, you know.

SHELLY. Enlighten me.

JILL. All of a sudden, I'm a threat.

SHELLY. You, a threat? To what?

JILL. You and Mark.

SHELLY. What?

JILL. Sure. Russ and I break up, suddenly you've got failure close up. Like lightning zapped us and you've got the smell of it in your nostrils. And if it could happen to us, if we could get zapped, who knows who could be zapped next?

SHELLY. Maybe we're more secure than you think.

JILL. Could you possibly be a little more smug?

SHELLY. I get the weirdest feeling that you want me to apologize to you for something. I can't for the life of me think what. Is it that I'm not miserable? Does misery really love company so much that if I'm not in pain you feel like I'm betraying you somehow? What would make you happier? If I confessed to you that I was having an affair? Or that he beat me or that we take turns having sex with the dog?

JILL. Enough. Sorry. It's just, yeah, it is a little oppressive being around people who get along as well as you guys.

SHELLY. It's not all *Donna Reed*.

JILL. No, but still you've got something that seems to work. And here I am on the verge of — oh Christ, I don't want to be one of that sad-eyed crowd of disconnected ladies. I don't want to have to learn how to say, "No, I really *enjoy* having my own space." Talking about how much reading I get done. And how *much* I've learned about myself by living alone. I know enough about myself to know that I don't want to know all that much more.

SHELLY. Oh, come on, Jill —

JILL. Loneliness is not an opportunity. It is not a growing experience. It's just fucking lonely.

SHELLY. Well, don't give up so quickly.

JILL. It's not a matter of *my* giving up. You're forgetting, Russ has taken off —

SHELLY. Actually, he called. *(A beat.)*

JILL. What?

SHELLY. Russ. He called this morning.

JILL. Why didn't you tell me before?

SHELLY. Just mean I guess. *(A beat.)*

JILL. What did he say?

SHELLY. Well, he asked for you.

JILL. What did you say?

SHELLY. That you were off with a bank robber enjoying

53

some standard-issue sex.

JILL.   Please —

SHELLY.   I said you went for a drive, you said to think things through.

JILL.   And?

SHELLY.   He asked how you were.

JILL.   Do I have to pull this out of you word-by-word?

SHELLY.   OK, he said he thought maybe he'd screwed up big-time.

JILL.   So, I was right. There *is* somebody else?

SHELLY.   That was the pretty clear implication —

JILL.   Who?

SHELLY.   I didn't press him on it.

JILL.   I'll bet it's Nancy Latham. I'll just bet it's Nancy Latham. She's got tits and whenever we're at a party together she tells me how lucky I am.

SHELLY.   He didn't say. And if I were you, when he gets here I wouldn't bring it up.

JILL.   Wait, wait, hold on. When he gets here? He's coming here?

SHELLY.   That's part of why he called. To say that he was on his way up. To make sure you'd be here to come up to.

JILL.   When?

SHELLY.   He's driving from the city. That's — what? — a little less than a two-hour drive? And he called, I guess forty-five minutes ago.

JILL.   You told him that it was OK?

SHELLY.   It's not my place to say whether it's OK or not. He has a half-share in this house this week, he has the right —

JILL.   And besides, since he's an old friend of yours —

SHELLY.   Excuse me, but what do you think you're saying?

JILL.   Sorry, sorry, sorry.

SHELLY.   I was under the impression you'd like him back. Am I wrong? That you don't want to be — disconnected I think is what you —

JILL.   Yeah, but on what terms?

SHELLY.   Well, I guess that's what you two have to talk about. I am not offering myself as a mediator or a counselor. But my completely unsolicited opinion: it's worth a try. In my experience, sometimes the difference between something working and not working can be whether one person is smart enough not to say something they have every right to say but that could only do damage.

JILL.   That one person in this case being me?

SHELLY.   Just because you have ammunition doesn't mean you have to use it. Do you want to score every point you can score, or do you want to —

JILL.   OK, OK, I get the drift. I do.

SHELLY.   I'd *prefer* it if you two stay together. I get tired of pencilling in corrections in my phone book.

JILL.   So we should stay together as a favor to you. Aside from any cornball considerations like love.

SHELLY.   Hey, have you heard me use the word?

JILL.   Did he sound miserable?

SHELLY.   Russ?

JILL.   Tell me he sounded miserable.

SHELLY.   Do you want me to lie?

JILL.   Do you have to?

SHELLY.   No. Not really.

JILL.   You've known him. You've known him for years.

SHELLY.   And it's on the basis of that I think it's worth it.

JILL.   God, I'm so confused. *(Mark enters through the door wearing a bathrobe. He indeed has a shiner.)* You're out of the shower.

MARK.   There's still plenty of hot water. In case *you're* thinking of taking a shower. Which personally I would recommend.

SHELLY.   *(Cautioning.)* Mark —

MARK.   *(To Shelly.)* Don't you think that would be a good idea? You did tell her that Russ is on his way over.

JILL.   I heard, yes.

MARK.   Not that your hygiene is my business —

SHELLY.   Mark, please —

JILL.   Look, you're pissed and you have a right to be.

MARK.   Yes, I do.

JILL.   I shouldn't have slugged you.

MARK.   Don't you think it would be better now if I *hadn't* given you the keys?

JILL.   Why can't we say the whole thing was real unfortunate and move forward?

MARK.   Here's the thing about that word "unfortunate": It
implies that fortune — luck, happenstance — had something
to do with what went on. That events were somehow outside
your control. You didn't *do* anything. Things *happened* to you.
You didn't make any choices. This huge boulder of circumstance bore down on you and poor you, you just couldn't get
out of the way.

JILL.   What is this — the relay scolding team? Shelly already
worked me over pretty good, you know.

SHELLY.   I did, Mark. I spanked her good.

JILL.   And I am sorry I hit you.

MARK.   Fuck being hit. Who cares? Fine. It doesn't matter.
That really doesn't matter. The bigger thing that I'm concerned about is Russ is going to show up pretty soon and
you're going to ask us not to say anything.

SHELLY.   Why should we say anything?

JILL.   Why should you say anything?

SHELLY.   When he called and asked for her, I said she was
upset and took her car out. I did not lie to him.

MARK.   Oh no, it's not lying to not say something. I see.
It's not lying.

JILL.   Mark, what is your problem?

MARK.   My problem is that you went out and spent the night
with this guy.

JILL.   You don't know that. You don't know what I did.
You're assuming.

MARK.   Oh, give me credit, I'm assuming right.

JILL.   But you don't know. So if you don't know —

MARK.   Then what's your story? After you punched me and
took the keys? Where did you go? What did you do?

JILL.   I don't have to tell you that. Look, if I don't say anything, then you don't know anything, and then you don't have
to lie.

MARK.   Deniability, hunh? What — did you intern in the
Bush White House?

JILL.   You self-righteous son-of-a-bitch, why are you doing this? Why are you attacking me?

MARK. *(Raising his voice for the first time.)* Because you did the wrong thing! You did the wrong thing! What you did was wrong! It was not the correct thing to do!

JILL. And you never did anything like this? You never picked up somebody? You never — with somebody you met in a bar or at a party — ?

MARK. Not while I was married.

JILL. Well, last night I didn't know whether or not I was still married. I did not know that.

MARK. So you don't know where you stand for a few hours and that gives you license to —

JILL. *(Over.)* Why can Russ go off with somebody and I can't?

MARK. I'm not suggesting that he can —

JILL. I don't see you hollering about Russ.

MARK. Russ isn't here for me to holler at.

JILL. Like you would.

SHELLY. Time out! Time out! Can I ask a simple — What are we going to do when Russ gets here?

MARK. *(At the top of his lungs.) Good question!* Just what I'm asking! *(A beat.)*

SHELLY. I want to apologize for my husband.

MARK. You haven't got the right to apologize for me. If I do something wrong, it's up to me to apologize. And I'm not, and I won't. *(A beat.)*

SHELLY. *(Gently.)* Jill, why don't you go inside? Do what you have to do.

JILL. *(Near tears.)* Shelly, please don't let him —

SHELLY. Don't worry.

JILL. Please.

SHELLY. Go inside now. Take care of yourself. Go on. *(Jill hesitates, then goes inside. A beat. Shelly turns on Mark.)* I'm not recognizing you. *(A beat.)*

MARK. What do you propose?

SHELLY. That we give them a chance. Jesus Christ, it's hard enough for people to manage. Why do you have to make it harder?

MARK. And so they make up —

SHELLY. I hope they do —

MARK. And what? We just go on? The four of us? Dinners, drinks, arguing about the Op-Ed page like nothing's happened? How are we supposed to do that?

SHELLY. We just will. Get over it. Live with it. There's a friend of yours that called me one night when his wife was out of town, told me he wasn't wearing anything and could I picture that? You think I don't think of that every time I see him?

MARK. Who?

SHELLY. I'm not going to tell you. Forget it. Get over it. It's meaningless.

MARK. I don't think it *is* meaningless. I'm sorry, I think this is exactly the stuff that does have meaning.

SHELLY. It must be awfully lonely for you — by yourself on top of that mountain.

MARK. I didn't think I was by myself. I thought that you and I basically believed the same things.

SHELLY. I thought so, too. I guess we've learned something.

MARK. I guess so. *(A beat.)* I've spent years feeling vaguely guilty about breaking up with her. And it always comes up. Not directly usually. Sometimes it's a joke. But — spoken or unspoken — the accusation that I'm responsible for what's become of her. If I hadn't called it quits all those years ago —

SHELLY. You're tired of it.

MARK. I'm real tired of it.

SHELLY. So this is what? You getting even?

MARK. No.

SHELLY. Are you sure? *(A beat.)* What if I tell you that she told me nothing happened?

MARK. Last night?

SHELLY. What if I tell you that she caught up with that guy, and he was so upset by you bursting in on them that he told her that it wasn't worth the trouble?

MARK. And she didn't come home until this morning?

SHELLY. She was angry, she was embarrassed. She slept in her car.

MARK. She'd rather that I think she spent the night with

58

that character than tell me that?

SHELLY.   Think about it.

MARK.   But why would that be —

SHELLY.   Think about it. You're a smart guy. You're a sensitive man. Think about it.

MARK.   Well, I guess I can see how that —

SHELLY.   You can't let her know that I told you. It's important to her.

MARK.   She said this to you? That this is what happened?

SHELLY.   Yes. *(A beat.)*

MARK.   OK. *(A beat.)*

SHELLY.   I figure tonight I can make the roast.

MARK.   Yeah, that sounds good. That could work. *(Fade out.)*

NOTES

There is no rule that says how plays must be built.

Yes, I do believe there are craft principles of dramatic writing that one ignores at one's peril. I wrote a book called *The Dramatist's Toolkit* (published by Heinemann) to articulate these principles as I understand them and apply them in my own work.

But the fact that the vast majority of contemporary plays are written by single writers at keyboards doesn't mean that every script has to be generated in this way. *With and Without* is a case in point.

I used to be associated with Alice's Fourth Floor, a small theater on 42nd Street's Theater Row. When I floated the proposition of working improvisationally with member artists, Susann Brinkley, the space's artistic director, offered me a weekly slot to give it a try.

The first thing I had to do was to establish some common language with the actors and writers who joined me. Theatrical improvisation is not simply a matter of actors leaping onto a stage and blurting out whatever occurs to them. Just as jazz musicians must be familiar with key signatures, meters, and have some working knowledge of the principles of harmony and counterpoint, so improvisational actors work from a set of shared understandings.

In an interview I did with longtime improvisational actor-director Del Close (which appears in my book on Second City, *Something Wonderful Right Away*), Del summarized what he saw as the theoretical underpinnings of the work:

"1. Don't deny verbal reality. If it's said, it's real. 'What about our children?' 'We don't have any.' That's wrong. Same is true with physical reality. If another actor physically establishes something, it is there and you mustn't do anything that says it's not there.

"2. Take the active as opposed to the passive choice. Of course, this means a great deal. It means you are free to choose on a stage. Which, if you choose to ponder that for a second, means you are in an existentialist state of living your life in public.

"3. The actor's business is to justify. What this came out of was a time when one of the actresses in [the] St. Louis [company of the Compass Players] said, 'The character I'm playing in the scene wouldn't *do* that. How can I justify doing that?' Elaine [May]'s response: 'The actor's job *is* to justify.'"

(If you're interested in more of Del's ideas, *Something Wonderful* has been reprinted by Limelight Editions, and Meriwether Publishing has released a book called *Truth in Comedy* by Del, Charna Halpern and Kim "Howard" Johnson. I also recommend Viola Spolin's pioneering *Improvisation for the Theatre* and, for a British perspective, Keith Johnstone's *Impro*.)

Various improvisational companies, directors and teachers over the years have invented hundreds of theater games — structures that enable actors to spontaneously and cooperatively generate theatrical activity. I drew on some of these games to develop the common language I needed the members of my workshop to speak.

I'm not going to pretend that a few weeks of playing the games turned us into demon improvisers who could hold our own at Second City, but we began to be able to listen to each other and build scenes jointly.

"Jointly" is an important word. One of the key distinctions between working improvisationally and writing at your desk is that the former is a social activity and the latter is not. Working alone, of course, you have complete control over what you produce. This also means that you have only your own resources on which to draw.

Working improvisationally, you must give up your authorial control in order to have the benefit of the creative resources of the group. Though an improvisational scene may have its genesis in an individual's idea, when you're genuinely improvising, everyone present has a determining influence on the action.

For example, you might begin by setting up and playing a simple courtship scene set in a restaurant. Then another actor may come in and introduce an additional element that changes its direction — say that because of a flash flood the restaurant is surrounded by water, and nobody will be able to leave until tomorrow morning. You may continue to play the courtship scene, but it necessarily will be influenced by the changed circumstance. (It is a complete coincidence that as I write this I am sitting in Key West surrounded by tropical storm Florence.)

There are different ways improvisation may be employed to develop material. During their run in Chicago with the Compass Players, Paul Sills, David Shepherd, Mike Nichols, Elaine May, Severn Darden, Barbara Harris, Shelley Berman, Walter Beakel, Mark and Barbara Gordon and the others would begin with scenarios similar to those that were employed in the *commedia dell'arte*. These scenarios were essentially outlines describing the action of a piece.

For instance, Paul Sills's outline for "The Game of Hurt" (dating from the mid-Fifties) told the story of a man who, mean and drunk in a Chicago bar, sells his wife to a young steelworker. (Sills says he got the idea from Thomas Hardy's novel *The Mayor of Casterbridge.*) Dismayed by her husband's behavior, the wife actually goes off with the steelworker, who turns out to be a nice, lonely guy. Sober the next morning, the abashed and embarrassed husband tries to get her to return to him.

Sills did not write any dialogue, but this outline set up circumstances to stimulate the actors' invention. The company improvised their way through the piece a couple of times and then put it up in front of an audience. The lines, of course, were not set, but the actions were. So the actors played the piece's *actions,* and the dialogue was a by-product of their behavior.

As exhilarating as it may be to watch actors improvising their way through a scenario in performance, I am primarily a playwright, and my interest is in employing this process to arrive at a completed, playable script.

In the nature of an experiment, some years ago I wrote a short outline about a man named Frank whose best friend, Marty, tries to enlist him in a lie to his wife Diane to cover his (Marty's) infidelity. I turned on a tape recorder. Two friends and I improvised our way through the scene three times. I typed up transcripts, edited together the sections I liked most and interwove them with new material that occurred to me in revision. The result was a short piece called "Cover" which was published in Samuel French's *25 Ten-Minute Plays from Actors Theatre of Louisville,* has been produced dozens of times, and which Michael Bigelow Dixon (Louisville's literary manager) tells me he uses to demonstrate what can be accomplished in a short-short play.

Similarly I understand that *Hatful of Rain* started as an outline by Michael V. Gazzo. Gazzo knew what his story was before he gathered together a group of players from the Actors Studio, but the moment-to-moment specifics were discovered as his workshop cast improvised within the dramatic beats he had established. He then culled the best of what had been created and augmented it. The resulting script was produced on Broadway, where it was a hit, and then adapted for film.

In addition to bringing a premise to a group of improvisers, a playwright may find ideas in the middle of an improvisational session. This is what I was hoping would happen at Alice's.

And indeed one morning an idea presented itself. There were three men and two women present, and, trying to figure out a situation that would support this configuration, I proposed we play a scene about three couples who are in the habit of vacationing together. We've arrived at the house we've rented only to discover that one of the wives hasn't shown up and probably isn't going to show up. So the other two couples are left to cope with the abandoned husband.

No, the scene we played then was by no means a finished product, or even something that might have entertained an outside audience. But there was enough promise in what resulted that I thought there was a play to be developed out of it.

At this point, I stepped in as playwright and reorganized the material. Looking to write a small-cast play, I decided it would concern two couples, not three. Looking to write a play emphasizing good roles for actresses (it's no secret that there are fewer good roles for women than men), I decided that instead of a missing wife I would deal with a missing husband.

At that point, I began private improvisational sessions with two of the actresses, Beth Lincks and Kristine Niven. I would set up circumstances for scenes, and then the three of us would let fly with a tape recorder running.

I am not going to claim that a great deal of what we came up with in those three or four sessions ended up in the final script (maybe four or five pages in total out of the entire text), but I learned a lot about these characters and the quality of their relationships and their histories. I learned how they interact and what their differing philosophies are. And learning these things made it possible for me to create a plot to accommodate them. In so doing, I added the character of Glen.

There have now been a number of readings and performances of this play, and I have learned a few things about it that may be helpful to those who undertake it.

There is no danger that, with her marriage in doubt, Jill will end up in bed with Mark, nor does Shelly believe there is any such danger. Not that, if Shelly weren't in the picture, Jill wouldn't be interested, but Mark has vivid memories of Jill's volatility and has no interest whatsoever in exposing himself to more. He does care about her, and he does like her. Though, due to the circumstances, we don't see much of her happier side, at her best Jill is lively and funny and good, if exhausting, company. Ideally, hints of this other, more attractive side will bubble up from time to time. Jill is also the one character who swears without inhibition, and she uses her willingness to swear as a way of gaining advantage in conversation.

Mark likes to fancy himself the voice of reason. One of the reasons he is far better off with Shelly than he was with Jill is that Jill has the ability to trigger a temper he would much prefer to keep under wraps. In fact, it is only with Jill that Mark loses his temper in this play. He is also, yes, a little pompous, and this makes him a very tempting target of Jill and Shelly's teasing. (The difference in the teasing is that Shelly never crosses the border into an outright attack, and Jill sometimes does.) To say that he is pompous is not to say that he is without a sense of humor, and sometimes that humor is aimed at what he recognizes is his own tendency to act pompous. Mark is also fairly rigid in his values.

Shelly is more flexible. It's not that she's less principled, it's that flexibility is one of her principles. Part of the journey of the play involves her discovery that, as much as she loves Mark (and they do have a good marriage), their values are distinct. Shelly prizes kindness over strict honesty. (I suppose Shelly is more New Testament and Mark leans toward the Old.)

I've been intrigued by the different reactions the ending has triggered. While most people support Shelly's behavior, a vocal minority are upset by it. They think that the fact that she can lie to her husband prefigures the end of the marriage. I don't think so, and I would prefer the ending not be played with intimations of storm clouds. I do mean for the ending to be provocative.

About Glen. Truth to tell, I based this character on a friend, with his permission. (Yes, he did rob a bank with a starter's pistol and he did get sent to jail.) Glen is a literate, gentle guy, not some obvious stud. The scene between him and Jill is built on a few different levels.

On the most obvious level, it is a mutual seduction by two bruised and cautious people. They both have been out of the mating dance for so long that they are awkward and unsure. Actors playing the scene must register not only the discomfort but the attempt to hide the discomfort from each other.

While much of what is going on is a woman and a man talking each other and themselves into bed, a substantial chunk has a decidedly non-sexual aspect. As Glen talks about some of what he has done and gone through because of a divorce he didn't want, Jill can't help but look at him as someone who has taken a path she is afraid she may have to follow. In these passages, Glen is figuratively standing next to her, pointing out some of the landmarks of the world of which she may soon become a citizen.

The third level is one of class. Jill wants this to work out, so she's not going to make too big a point of the difference in their social status, but the difference is there and she doesn't mind if he is aware of it. He is a carpenter. She doesn't have much dealings with the carpenters who work on the projects she organizes. Though not wealthy herself, she is accustomed to moving easily among wealthy people. He has had little contact with that class. He's spent almost all of his life in the small towns along the Hudson, and, yes, because of economic circumstances, he does indeed live in a trailer. But he is not the yokel Jill has assumed him to be. He went to a small college, he reads and he can form original thoughts. Though Jill begins the scene subtextually indicating to him that he's gotten lucky tonight and that ordinarily he wouldn't have much of a chance with someone of her situation, she gradually begins to realize that they are both lucky in their choice of companions for the evening.

This scene is also the best chance we have to see Jill's more appealing side. She may frequently be overwhelming, but there is something there with which a self-respecting man could fall in love.

If this play is played the way I intend it, there are no villains. These are all good people of different temperaments trying their best to stay afloat. It is the difference in their temperaments that leads to the problems they need to resolve.

One final note on the playing. This is not intended as a slam-bang comedy. There are very few one-liners here. The humor comes primarily out of behavior and not language. The more simply and honestly this is played, the funnier it will be.

Incidentally, a cassette of the radio version, recorded by Chicago Theatres on the Air in front of a live audience, is available for purchase. Directed by Sandy Shinner, who also directed the Chicago stage premiere, it stars Lindsay Crouse as Jill, Michael Tucker as Mark, Jill Eikenberry as Shelly and Tim Halligan as Glen, and I am very pleased with it. Copies may be ordered with a credit card by phoning Los Angeles Theatre Works at 1-800-708-8863.

PROPERTY LIST

Nerf gun with sponges (JILL)
Wicker hamper (SHELLY) with:
       bottle of wine
       2 wine glasses
Binoculars (MARK)
Paperback book (JILL)
Purse with keys (JILL)
Bottle of wine (JILL)
Sunglasses (JILL)
Wallet with photograph (GLEN)
Boom box (JILL)
Reading material (SHELLY)
Orange juice (JILL)
Drinking glasses (JILL)

SOUND EFFECTS

Distant laughter
Slow, romantic music
Car starting and driving away

TODAY'S HOTTEST NEW PLAYS

❑ **MOLLY SWEENEY by Brian Friel, Tony Award-Winning Author of** *Dancing at Lughnasa.* Told in the form of monologues by three related characters, *Molly Sweeney* is mellifluous, Irish storytelling at its dramatic best. Blind since birth, Molly recounts the effects of an eye operation that was intended to restore her sight but which has unexpected and tragic consequences. *"Brian Friel has been recognized as Ireland's greatest living playwright. Molly Sweeney confirms that Mr. Friel still writes like a dream. Rich with rapturous poetry and the music of rising and falling emotions...Rarely has Mr. Friel written with such intoxicating specificity about scents, colors and contours."* - New York Times. [2M, 1W]

❑ **SWINGING ON A STAR (The Johnny Burke Musical) by Michael Leeds. 1996 Tony Award Nominee for Best Musical.** The fabulous songs of Johnny Burke are perfectly represented here in a series of scenes jumping from a 1920s Chicago speakeasy to a World War II USO Show and on through the romantic high jinks of the Bob Hope/Bing Crosby "Road Movies." Musical numbers include such favorites as "Pennies from Heaven," "Misty," "Ain't It a Shame About Mame," "Like Someone in Love," and, of course, the Academy Award winning title song, "Swinging on a Star." *"A WINNER. YOU'LL HAVE A BALL!"* - New York Post. *"A dazzling, toe-tapping, finger-snapping delight!"* - ABC Radio Network. *"Johnny Burke wrote his songs with moonbeams!"* - New York Times. [3M, 4W]

❑ **THE MONOGAMIST by Christopher Kyle.** Infidelity and mid-life anxiety force a forty-something poet to reevaluate his 60s values in a late 80s world. *"THE BEST COMEDY OF THE SEASON. Trenchant, dark and jagged. Newcomer Christopher Kyle is a playwright whose social satire comes with a nasty, ripping edge - Molière by way of Joe Orton."* - Variety. *"By far the most stimulating playwright I've encountered in many a buffaloed moon."* - New York Magazine. *"Smart, funny, articulate and wisely touched with rue...the script radiates a bright, bold energy."* - The Village Voice. [2M, 3W]

❑ **DURANG/DURANG by Christopher Durang.** These cutting parodies of *The Glass Menagerie* and *A Lie of the Mind,* along with the other short plays in the collection, prove once and for all that Christopher Durang is our theater's unequivocal master of outrageous comedy. *"The fine art of parody has returned to theater in a production you can sink your teeth and mind into, while also laughing like an idiot."* - New York Times. *"If you need a break from serious drama, the place to go is Christopher Durang's silly, funny, over-the-top sketches."* - TheatreWeek. [3M, 4W, flexible casting]

DRAMATISTS PLAY SERVICE, INC.
440 Park Avenue South, New York, New York 10016 212-683-8960 Fax 212-213-1539

TODAY'S HOTTEST NEW PLAYS

❏ **THREE VIEWINGS by Jeffrey Hatcher.** Three comic-dramatic monologues, set in a midwestern funeral parlor, interweave as they explore the ways we grieve, remember, and move on. *"Finally, what we have been waiting for: a new, true, idiosyncratic voice in the theater. And don't tell me you hate monologues; you can't hate them more than I do. But these are much more: windows into the deep of each speaker's fascinating, paradoxical, unique soul, and windows out into a gallery of surrounding people, into hilarious and horrific coincidences and conjunctions, into the whole dirty but irresistible business of living in this damnable but spellbinding place we presume to call the world." - New York Magazine.* [1M, 2W]

❏ **HAVING OUR SAY by Emily Mann.** The Delany Sisters' Bestselling Memoir is now one of Broadway's Best-Loved Plays! Having lived over one hundred years apiece, Bessie and Sadie Delany have plenty to say, and their story is not simply African-American history or women's history...it is our history as a nation. *"The most provocative and entertaining family play to reach Broadway in a long time." - New York Times. "Fascinating, marvelous, moving and forceful." - Associated Press.* [2W]

❏ **THE YOUNG MAN FROM ATLANTA Winner of the 1995 Pulitzer Prize. by Horton Foote.** An older couple attempts to recover from the suicide death of their only son, but the menacing truth of why he died, and what a certain Young Man from Atlanta had to do with it, keeps them from the peace they so desperately need. *"Foote ladles on character and period nuances with a density unparalleled in any living playwright." - NY Newsday.* [5M, 4W]

❏ **SIMPATICO by Sam Shepard.** Years ago, two men organized a horse racing scam. Now, years later, the plot backfires against the ringleader when his partner decides to come out of hiding. *"Mr. Shepard writing at his distinctive, savage best." - New York Times.* [3M, 3W]

❏ **MOONLIGHT by Harold Pinter.** The love-hate relationship between a dying man and his family is the subject of Harold Pinter's first full-length play since *Betrayal*. *"Pinter works the language as a master pianist works the keyboard." - New York Post.* [4M, 2W, 1G]

❏ **SYLVIA by A.R. Gurney.** This romantic comedy, the funniest to come along in years, tells the story of a twenty-two year old marriage on the rocks, and of Sylvia, the dog who turns it all around. *"A delicious and dizzy new comedy." - New York Times. "FETCHING! I hope it runs longer than Cats!" - New York Daily News.* [2M, 2W]

DRAMATISTS PLAY SERVICE, INC.
440 Park Avenue South, New York, New York 10016 212-683-8960 Fax 212-213-1539